MW01224429

AUSTRALIA
small book big island

First published in Australia in 2014
by Craftsman House
an imprint of Thames & Hudson Australia Pty Ltd
11 Central Boulevard Portside Business Park
Port Melbourne Victoria 3207
ABN: 72 004 751 964

www.thameshudson.com.au

ISBN: 978 0 9873927 2 5

National Library of Australia Cataloguing-in-Publication entry

  Australia : small book, big island.
  9780987392725 (hardback)
    Landscape photography--Australia.
    Nature photography--Australia.
    Australia--Pictorial works.
919.4

Design: Susan Hardjono
Printed and bound in China by 1010 Printing

24th November 2016

Gernot,
A small token to remember
our beautiful country and hope
one day you come back!!
Kathy & Hans

small book

AUSTRALIA

big island

CRAFTSMAN HOUSE

NEW SOUTH WALES

AUSTRALIAN CAPITAL TERRITORY

VICTORIA

TASMANIA

SOUTH AUSTRALIA

WESTERN AUSTRALIA

NORTHERN TERRITORY

QUEENSLAND

NEW SOUTH WALES

~~~~~~~~~

Land size	800,642 km²
Population	7.52 million
Capital city	Sydney
Known for	beaches, fashion, fireworks
Main attractions	Sydney Opera House, Bondi Beach, Blue Mountains

New South Wales, Sydney

New South Wales Sydney Harbour

New South Wales Circular Quay

New South Wales Sydney Opera House

Queen Victoria Building · New South Wales

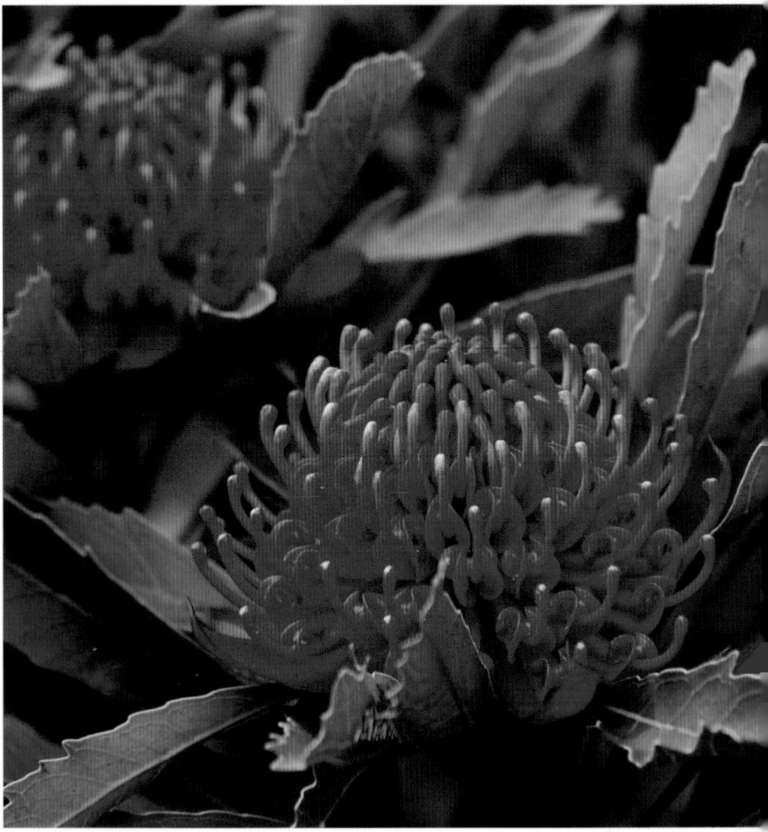

New South Wales Mardi Gras in central Sydney

New South Wales Ocean swim at Manly Beach

ice cream truck at Cronulla Beach New South Wales

New South Wales Sea Cliff Bridge, Clifton

New South Wales Coolamine Homestead, Snowy Mountains

New South Wales Coastal rock formations, Kiama

New South Wales Lord Howe Island

New South Wales Leura Falls, Blue Mountains

New South Wales **Blue Mountains**

AUSTRALIAN
CAPITAL TERRITORY

~~~~~~~

Land size	2,358 km²
Population	386,000
Capital city	Canberra
Known for	politics, art, roundabouts
Main attractions	Parliament House, Australian War Memorial, National Gallery of Australia

Victoria **Canberra**

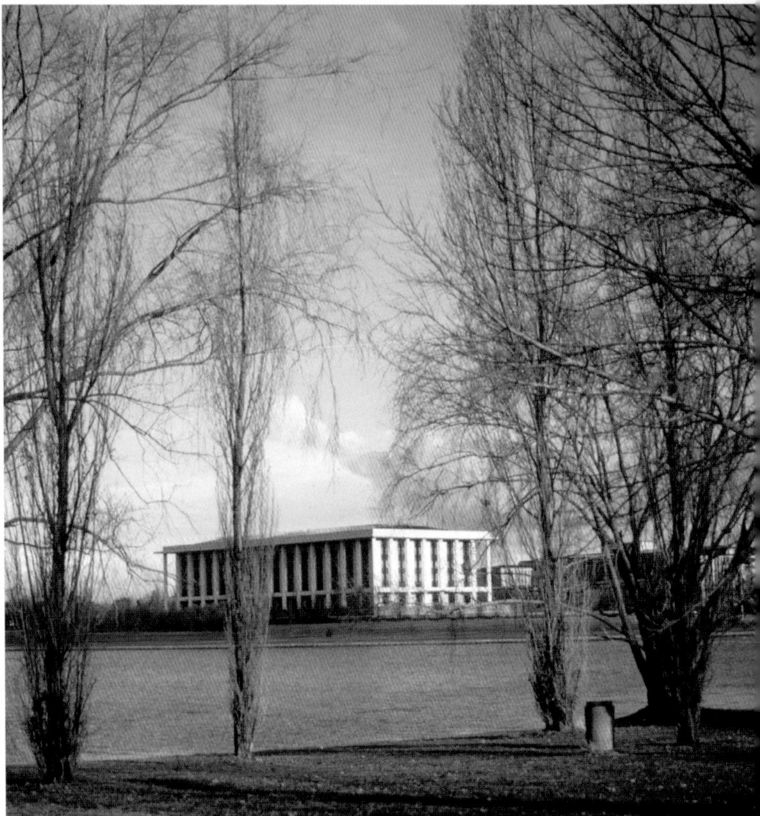

ACT National Library and Lake Burley Griffin

ACT Australian War Memorial

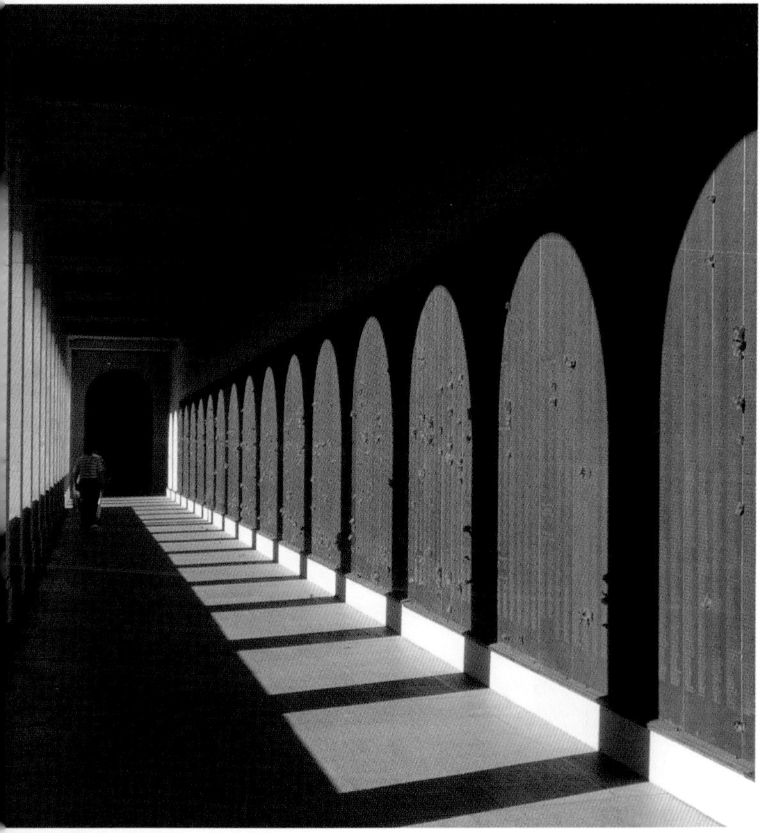

Australian War Memorial ACT

VICTORIA

Land size | 227,416 km²
Population | 5.84 million
Capital city | Melbourne
Known for | football, food, festivals
Main attractions | Federation Square, laneways,
Great Ocean Road

Victoria Melbourne

Victoria Federation Square

National Gallery of Victoria Victoria

Victoria Hosier Lane

Melbourne Central   Victoria

Victoria Fitzroy

St Kilda Pier Victoria

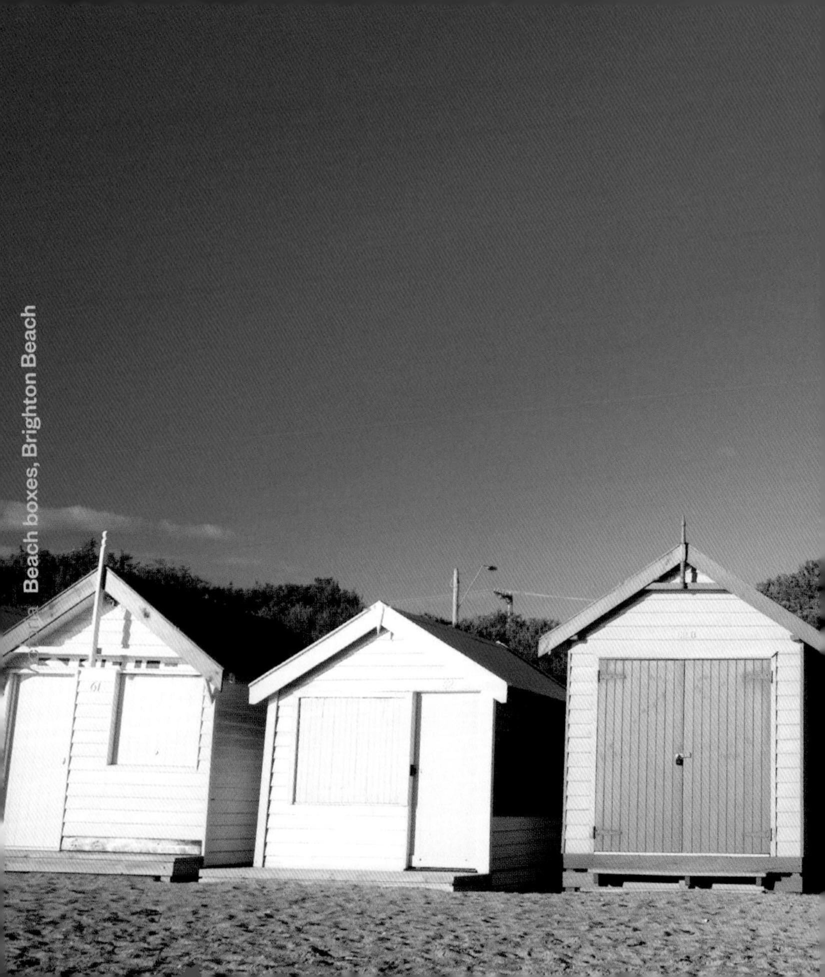

Beach boxes, Brighton Beach

Victoria **Bells Beach, Torquay**

Penguins, Philip Island Victoria

Victoria Wilsons Promontory National Park

Lerderderg State Park, Greendale Victoria

Victoria Koala

Victoria **Twelve Apostles, Port Campbell National Park**

Victoria Puffing Billy, Dandenong Ranges

Victoria Sovereign Hill, Ballarat

TASMANIA

Land size	68,401 km²
Population	514,800
Capital city	Hobart
Known for	heritage buildings, hiking, wilderness
Main attractions	MONA, Port Arthur, Salamanca Place

Tasmania: Hobart

Tasmania Victoria Dock, Hobart

Salamanca Market, Hobart, Tasmania

Tasmania MONA, Hobart

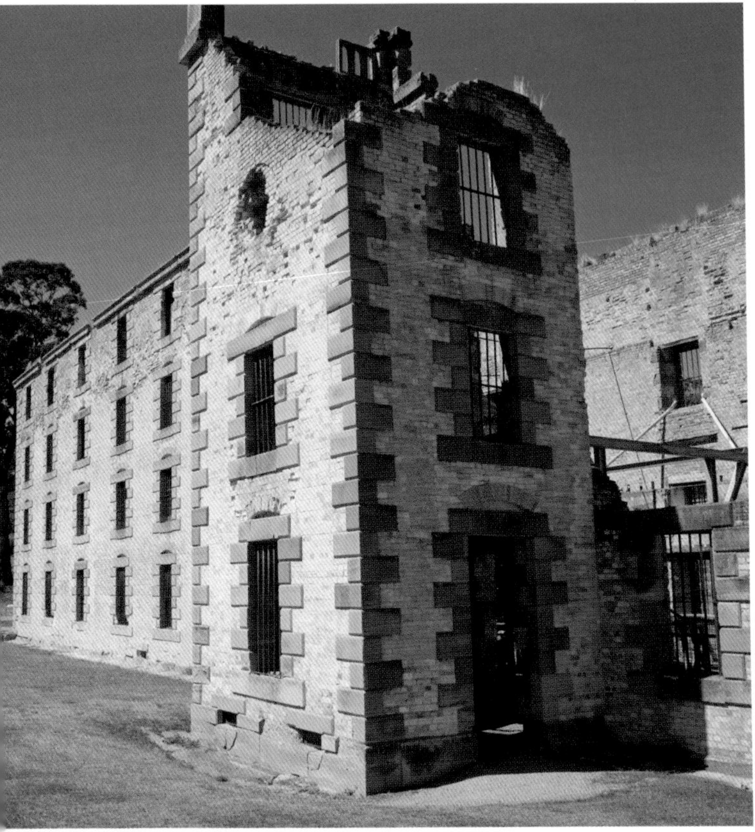

Historic former prison at Port Arthur Tasmania

Tasmania Cottage, Battery Point

Forest at the base of Mount Wellington, Tasmania

Cape Wickham Lighthouse, King Island Tasmania

Tasmania Red lichen on rock, Wineglass Bay

Tasmania · Cradle Mountain–Lake St Clair National Park

Tasmania Cradle Mountain

Gordon River Tasmania

Tasmania   Tasmanian Devil

Woodland Overland Track · Tasmania

Mount Wellington lookout   Tasmania

SOUTH AUSTRALIA

~~~~~~~

Land Size 983,482 km²

Population 1.68 million

Capital city Adelaide

Known for wineries, deserts, opals

Main attractions Barossa Valley, Kangaroo Island,
Flinders Ranges

South Australia Adelaide Festival Centre forecourt

South Australia **Bottlebrush**

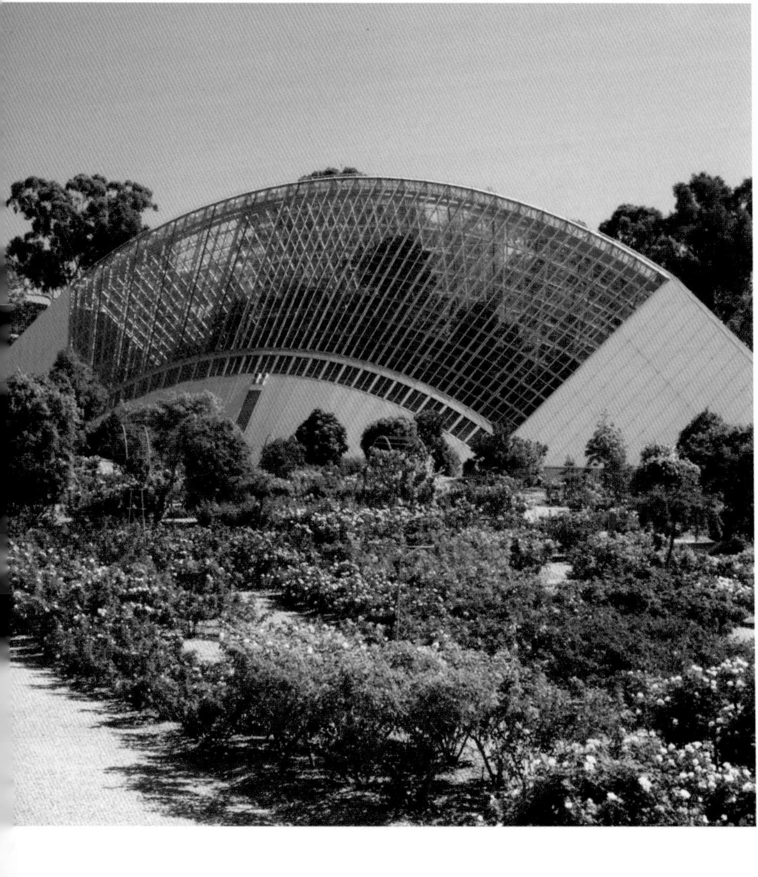

Adelaide Botanic Gardens South Australia

South Australia Red River Gum tree, Flinders Ranges

South Australia Sturt's Desert pea

Strzelecki Desert South Australia

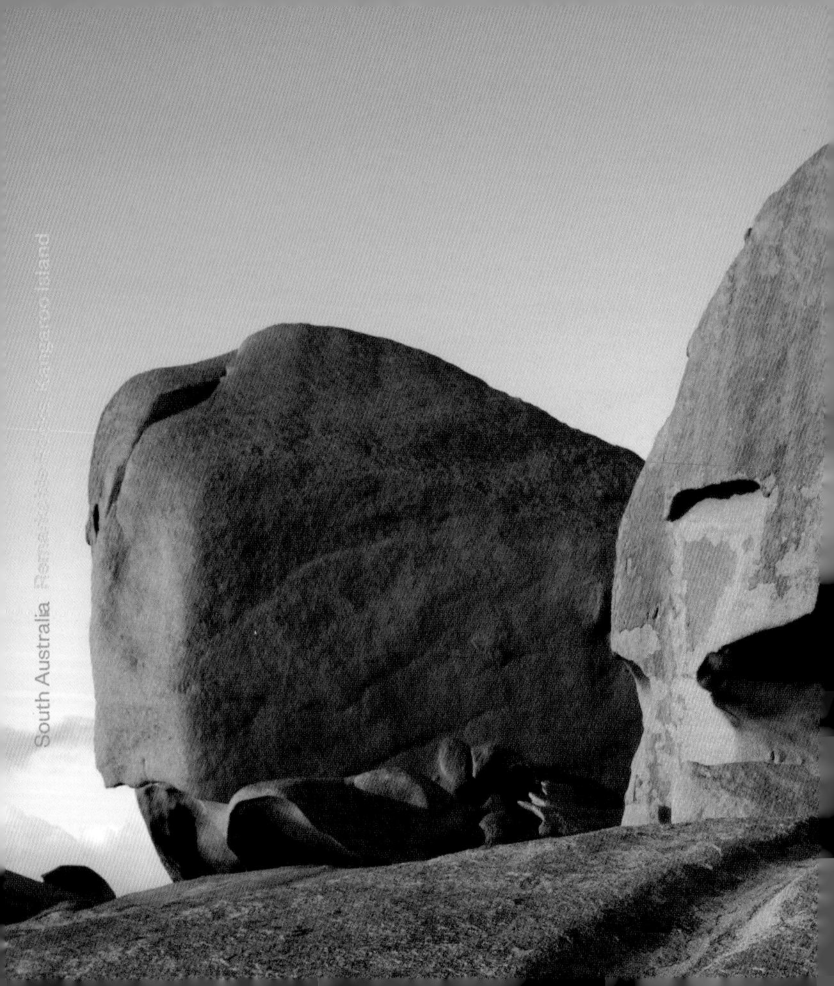

South Australia Remarkable Rocks Kangaroo Island

Australia Remarkable Rocks, Kangaroo Island

Seal Bay, Kangaroo Island South Australia

South Australia Kelly Hill Caves, Kangaroo Island

South Aust Barossa Valley Vineyard

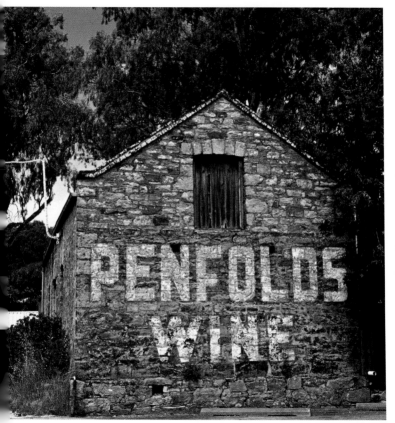

Penfolds Estate, Barossa Valley   South Australia

South Australia Morgan Beach, Cape Jervis

Glenelg Jetty

South Australia Crocodile Harry's garden, Coober Pedy

NEWLY PLANTED
LAWN
PLEASE
KEEP OFF

South Australia Nullarbor Plain

Mining truck sculpture in Coober Pedy South Australia

South Australia Miner's underground home, Coober Pedy

South Australia The Breakaways

WESTERN AUSTRALIA

~~~~~~~~

Land Size   2,529,875 km²

Population   2.57 million

Capital city   Perth

Known for   mining, crystal clear water,
                whale watching

Main attractions Margaret River, The Pinnacles,
                  Monkey Mia

Western Australia Little Creatures Brewery van

1897

MUNICIPAL COUNCIL

FREMANTLE

NEC PRECE NEC PRETIO

FREMANTLE

Monkey Mia Western Australia

Western Australia Quokkas

Yallingup

Western Australia The Bungle Bungles, Purnululu National Park

Picaninny Creek in Cathedral Gorge, Purnululu National Park,

Western Australia Limestone Pinnacles, Nambung National Park

Pinnacles Desert   Western Australia

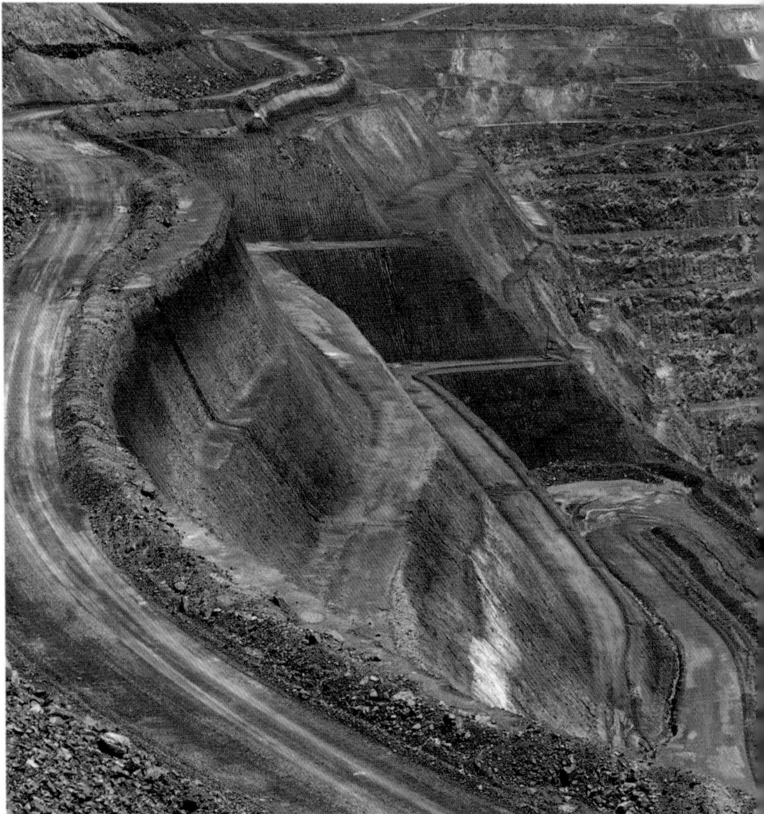

Western Australia Super Pit Gold Mine, Kalgoorlie

Gold prospector, Kalgoorlie, Western Australia

Historical bank converted into an outhouse, Croydon Western Australia

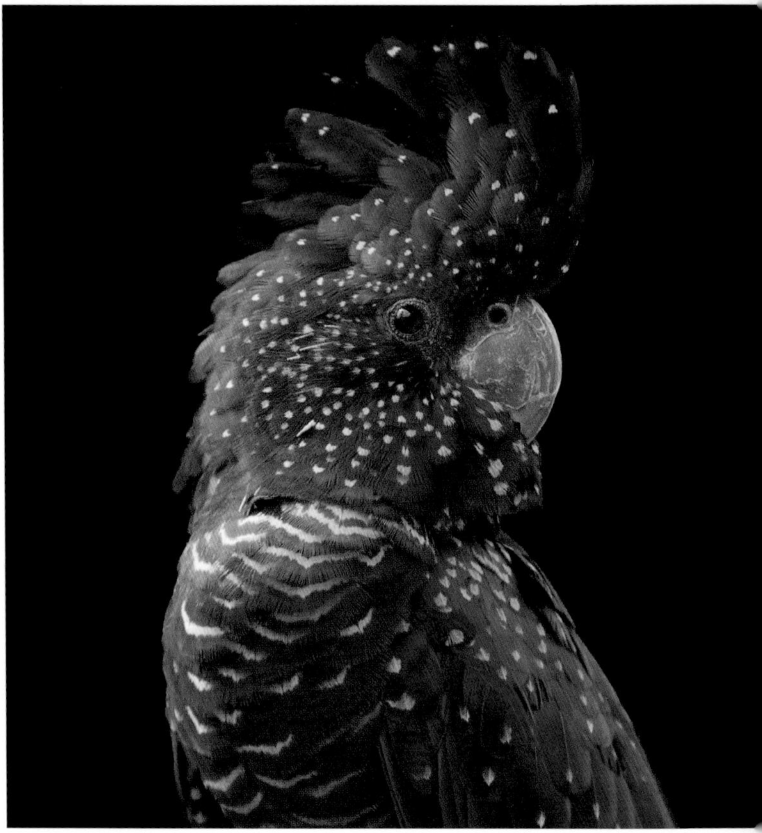

Western Australia Black Cockatoo

Mulla Mulla flowers

Wine barrels, Margaret River Western Australia

Western Australia Sunset camel ride, Cable Beach

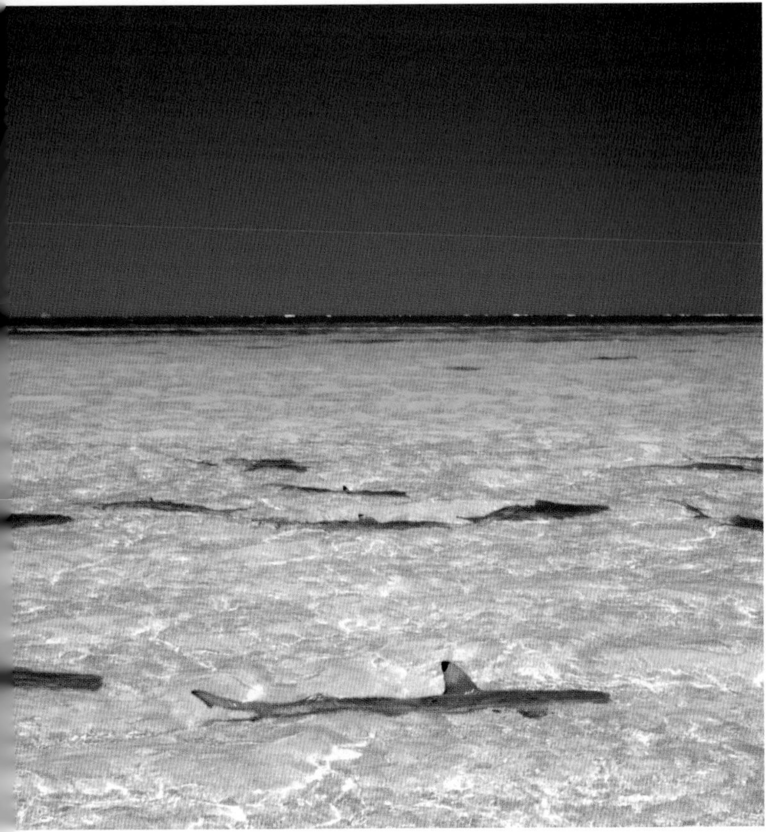

Young Lemon sharks, Perth Western Australia

Gibb River Road, Kimberly, Western Australia.

NORTHERN
TERRITORY

~~~~~~~~

Land Size · 1,349,129 km²

Population · 245,100

Capital city · Darwin

Known for · Indigenous culture, outback,
spectacular sunsets

Main attractions · Mary River, Uluru,
Kakadu National Park

Northern Territory Ghost Gum tree

Uluru and Yulara road sign Northern Territory

Northern Territory Aboriginal artist painting at Ngurratjuta Iltja Ntjarra

WELCOME TO
ALICE SPRINGS
TUNE TO 8?? FM FOR TOURIST INFORMATION

Northern Territory Emu

Nitmiluk Gorge

Northern Territory **Mini Palms Gorge**

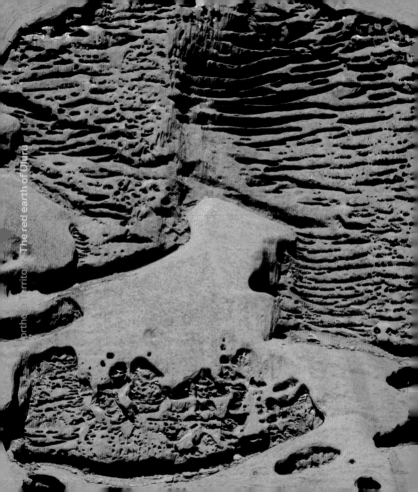

Uluru Northern Territory

Red crabs on Christmas Island

Northern Territory Nitmiluk National Park

Desert sand, Alice Springs Northern Territory

Northern Territory. Butterfly Gorge

George Gill Range near Kings Canyon Northern Territory

Northern Territory Mary River near Darwin

Northern Territory Mungo National Park

Northern Territory Katherine Gorge at Kakadu National Park

Northern Territory Edith Falls, Kakadu National Park

Black-necked Stork, Kakadu National Park Northern Territory

Northern Territory   Tributary to Twin Falls and Jim Jim Falls, Kakadu

QUEENSLAND

~~~~~~~~

Land size	1,730,648 km²
Population	4.72 million
Capital city	Brisbane
Known for	surfing, pristine beaches, rainforest
Main attractions	Sunshine Coast, Great Barrier Reef, The Whitsundays,

Queensland Brisbane River

Queensland Grand Arbour

Queensland Hill Inlet and Whitehaven Beach in Whitsunday Islands

Queensland Wet 'n' Wild theme park, Gold Coast

Fraser Island Queensland

Queensland Great Barrier Reef

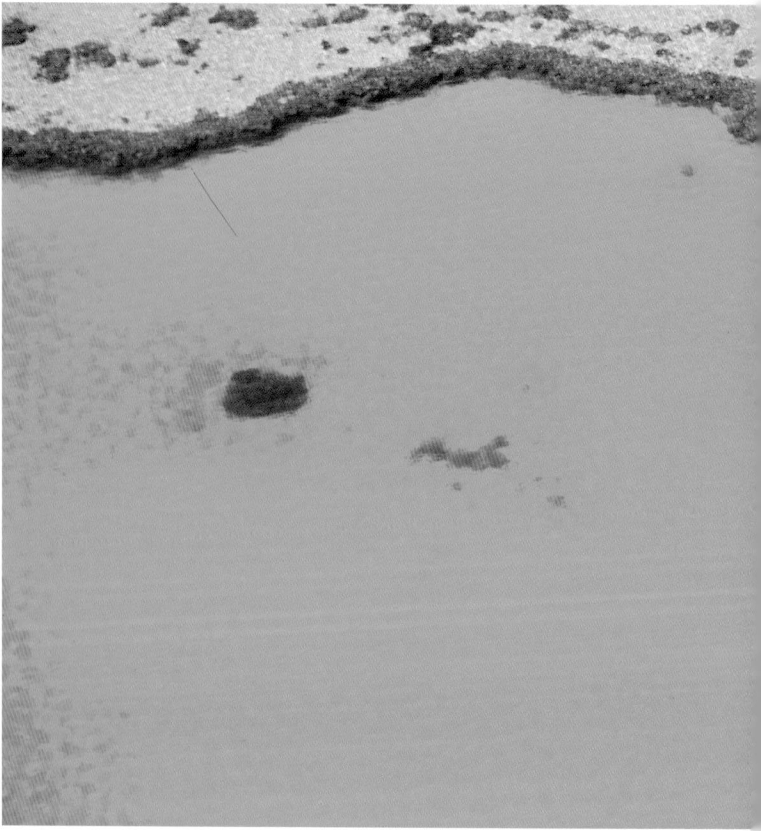

Queensland Heart Reef, Great Barrier Reef

Queensland Mackay

Mossman Gorge, Daintree National Park, Queensland

Queensland Daintree National Park

Queensland Mangroves, Daintree Rainforest

Aerial view of the rainforest near Cairns Queensland

Freshwater crocodiles

Dainty Tree Frog, Queensland

Queensland Flying Fox

Curtain Fig Tree, Daintree National Park Q

Queensland Barron Falls

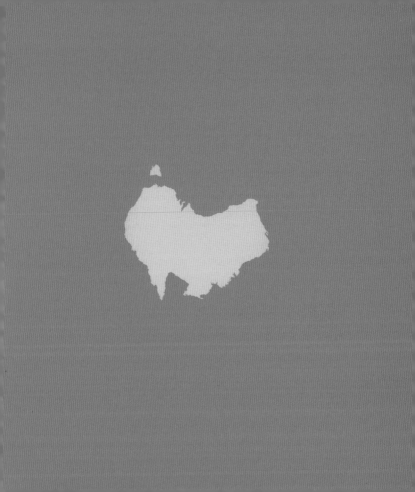

C/Christian Kober/Robert Harding World Imagery; C/Bill Hatcher/National Geographic Society; S/Bernhard Richter; S/Sasapee; S/Ian Woolcock; Brooke Holm; S/Ian Woolcock

SOUTH AUSTRALIA

C/Fridmar Dam; S/Timothy Craig Lubcke; S/Timothy Craig Lubcke; S/CTR Photos; S/Gary Unwin; S/Erena Wilson; C/DK Limited; C/Neale Clarke/Robert Harding World Imagery; S/Janelle Lugge; C/Martin Harvey; C/Konrad Wothe/Minden Pictures; C/Paul A. Souders; C/Geraint Tellem/Latitude Stock; S/Bernhard Richter; C/Neale Clarke/Robert Harding World Imagery; C/Nick Rains; C/Doug Pearson/JAI; C/Neale Clarke/Robert Harding World Imagery; C/Steve Parish Publishing; C/Andrew Watson/JAI; C/Howard Davies; C/Michael Runkel/Robert Harding World Imagery; C/Esther Beaton; S/Styve Reineck

WESTERN AUSTRALIA

S/Tupungato; C/Tom Morgan/Demotix; S/Daniel Lohmer; C/DK Limited; C/Roman Kalyakin/Demotix; Wee-Ching Kong; C/Ian Trower/Robert Harding World Imagery; S/attem; C/Roger Garwood & Trish Ainslie; C/Ian Trower/JAI; C/Jochen Schlenker/Robert Harding World Imagery; C/Ian Trower/Robert Harding World Imagery; C/Anne Montfort/Photononstop; C/Jochen Schlenker/Robert Harding World Imagery; C/Jochen Schlenker/Robert Harding World Imagery; C/Matthias Breiter/Minden Pictures; C/Ocean; C/B.Schmid/amanaimages; C/Paul A. Souders; C/Paul Mayall/dpa; C/Roger Garwood & Trish Ainslie; S/Edward Haylan; C/George Steinmetz; S/Markus Gebauer; S/Paul Looyen; C/Nick Rains; C/Andrew Watson/JAI; C/Ian Trower/Robert Harding World Imagery; C/Atlantide Phototravel; C/Doug Pearson/JAI; S/David Ashley; C/Descamps Simon/Hemis; C/Jochen Schlenker/Robert Harding World Imagery; C/David Samuel Robbins; C/Theo Allofs

NORTHERN TERRITORY

David Wall Photo; C/Momatiuk-Eastcott; C/John Van Hasselt/Sygma; C/Isabelle Vayron/Sygma; C/Andrew Watson/JAI; C/Paul A. Souders; C/Marianna Massey; S/NCG; S/Katherine Welles; Jesse Marlow; C/Radius Images; C/Tony Waltham/ Robert Harding World Imagery; C/Nick Rains; C/Paul A. Souders; C/Momatiuk-Eastcott; C/Roger Garwood & Trish Ainslie; C/Stephen Belcher/Foto Natura/Minden Pictures; C/Jason Edwards/National Geographic Society; C/Seiji Shimizu; C/Marianna Massey; C/Nick Rains; C/Gil Giuglio/Hemis; C/Stéphane Lemaire/Hemis; S/Manfred Kaempa; C/Nick Rains; C/Jan Butchofsky; C/Thomas Marent/Minden Pictures; C/Theo Allofs; C/Eric and David Hosking; S/BioLife Pics; S/EcoPrint; C/Robert Francis/Robert Harding World Imagery; C/Martin Willis/Minden Pictures; S/GTS Production

QUEENSLAND

S/Tupungato; S/wang song; C/Patrick Johns; S/chungking; S/Petronilo G. Dangoy Jr.; Gallery of Modern Art, Brisbane/Photograph: John Gollings /Image courtesy: Queensland Art Gallery | Gallery of Modern Art; Reko Rennie/Kamilaroi/Gamilaraay/Gummaroi peoples / Trust the 2% 2013 /Installation view of site-specific commission for 'My Country, I Still Call Australia Home: Contemporary Art from Black Australia at Gallery of Modern Art, Brisbane/Courtesy: The artist/Photograph: Natasha Harth/Image courtesy: Queensland Art Gallery | Gallery of Modern Art; C/Greg Probst; S/Steven Bostock; S/GTS Production; C/Andrew Watson/JAI; C/John Carnemolla; C/Lisa Wiltse; C/Lisa Wiltse; C/Matthew Williams-Ellis/Robert Harding World Imagery; S/GTS Production; C/Matthew Williams-Ellis/Robert Harding World Imagery; C/Matthew Williams-Ellis/Robert Harding World Imagery; C/Matthew Williams-Ellis; C/Atlantide Phototravel; C/Oliver Lucanus/Foto Natura/Minden Pictures; C/Doug Perrine/Design Pics; Corbis; C/Onne van der Wal; C/Nick Rains; S/hkomala; C/Peter Adams; C/Jochen Schlenker/Robert Harding World Imagery; S/Ralph Loesche; S/BioLife Pics; C/Peter Adams/JAI; S/Dirk Ercken; C/Ocean; C/Radius Images; C/Nick Servian/Robert Harding World Imagery; C/Michael Runkel/Robert Harding World Imagery; C/Gerry Ellis/Minden Pictures; C/Thomas Marent/Minden Pictures; C/Jochen Schlenker/Robert Harding World Imagery; S/Martin Froyda

C/ Corbis   S/ Shutterstock